Eyewitness
BIRD
Expert Files

Eyewitness
BIRD
Expert Files

DK Publishing, Inc.

LONDON, NEW YORK,
MELBOURNE, MUNICH, AND DELHI

Consultant Rob Hume
Senior Editor Jayne Miller
Project Editor Sarah Davis
Senior Art Editors Joanne Little, David Ball
Art Editors Owen Peyton Jones, Peter Radcliffe,
Susan St.Louis, Gemma Thompson
Paper Engineer Ruth Wickings
Managing Editor Camilla Hallinan
Art Director Martin Wilson
Publishing Manager Sunita Gahir
Category Publisher Andrea Pinnington
Picture Research Sarah Hopper
DK Picture Library Rose Horridge, Claire Bowers
Production Controller Angela Graef
DTP Designers Ronaldo Julien, Andy Hilliard
Jacket Designer Polly Appleton
Jacket Copywriter John Searcy

First published in the United States in 2007
by DK Publishing Limited,
375 Hudson Street, New York, New York 10014

07 08 09 10 11 10 9 8 7 6 5 4 3 2 1
ED511 – 07/07

A catalog record for this book is available
from the Library of Congress.

ISBN: 978–0–7566–3133–8

Color reproduction by Colourscan, Singapore
Printed and bound by Toppan Printing Co.
(Shenzhen) Ltd, China

**Discover more at
www.dk.com**

Contents

MEET THE EXPERTS

Experts who work with birds are known as ornithologists, but they do many and varied jobs. Meet a scientist who saves rare birds around the world, then find out about other types of bird experts and the way they work.

Ornithologist
EXPERT
PROFILE

NAME: **CHRIS BOWDEN**

LOCATION: **MOROCCO**

HOME COUNTRY: **BRITAIN**

Chris Bowden first started watching birds when he was eight years old. After studying ecology in college he joined the Royal Society for the Protection of Birds, working on projects to help safeguard endangered birds around the globe. His job has taken him to parts of Africa, India, North America, Syria, Romania, and the Caribbean. Between 1995 and 2003, he spent much of his time in Morocco researching and observing what was thought to be the last surviving wild population of Northern Bald Ibis left in the world.

CHRIS AND THE TEAM OF GARDIENS
Chris worked alongside a team of park wardens, or gardiens. Training the wardens was an important part of Chris's work, so they could take over monitoring the Ibis in the hope of saving the bird from dying out.

Saving the Bald Ibis

THIS DISTINCTIVE-LOOKING BIRD WAS ONCE
COMMON ALL OVER MOROCCO. NUMBERS
DWINDLED DRASTICALLY UNTIL THERE WERE
THOUGHT TO BE JUST 70 SURVIVING PAIRS OF
BIRDS—NO ONE REALLY KNEW WHY. OUR
EXPERT'S PROJECT WAS TO TRY AND SAVE A
SPECIES OF WILD BIRDS THAT WAS ON
THE BRINK OF BECOMING EXTINCT.

NORTHERN BALD IBIS
Known in Ancient Egypt,
Geronticus eremita, *or
the Northern Bald Ibis,
is a small, heron-like
bird with a bald
head and a long,
curved, red
beak.*

Spain

Morocco

ATLANTIC OCEAN

AFRICA

Souss-Massa
National Park

HOMING IN ON THE IBIS
*Morocco's Souss-Massa National Park is
on the northwest tip of Africa. It is home
to many rare and beautiful birds.*

Moroccan mission

When I started here in 1995, as far as I knew this was the only population of Bald Ibis in the world. There was a semiwild population in Turkey, and a Spanish zoo planned to release some back into the wild, although that's not always successful. My task was to watch and research the Ibises's feeding and breeding habits to find out factors that could be affecting them and make recommendations. I was here to save the Bald Ibis.

Chris with his trusty truck

The scenic coast of Morocco

Research and training

I work for BirdLife International and the British RSPB (Royal Society for the Protection of Birds). In Africa I worked with the Moroccan government and my role was a combination of scientific research and training lcoal park wardens to take over and continue the work when I had finished.

Daily schedule

I'd get up at 4 a.m. every morning to drive to the roost before the birds became active at dawn and began to leave for their feeding areas 15 miles (25 km) away. I'd head off in my trusty old Land Rover to follow the birds across the sand dunes and record where they fed and in what numbers. During the breeding season, it is crucial to check that they are safe, so I'd stay there all day. Every 10 minutes I'd note where they were feeding and mark it on a map. Ali Aghnaj, the deputy director for the national parks, came with me. The idea was to train local wardens on motorcycles to visit the locations and check the numbers of birds and their eating

BARREN LANDSCAPE
"It looks like the middle of nowhere, desert country," Chris says of the park. "But there are always people nearby, using the area, so we needed to gain their respect and support."

habits. It is very simple, but very important—it needs to be done.

Close up to the Ibis

While watching, you have to keep your distance, so that you don't disturb the birds—although they are very approachable when feeding. You have to be a shady figure, increasing your visibility gradually. I'm pretty sure the birds got to know me a bit over the years—and I feel that I got to know their characters!

A nearby raven nest—a threat to the Ibis

was an international business that didn't want the bad press—but local companies still need to do business and some development is inevitable. So we try to influence the way such plans take shape.

Although the park was set up to safeguard nesting areas, the Bald Ibises also feed on land outside the reserve, which is not effectively protected. Most Moroccans are unaware of the bird and the problems it faces. But then again, how many of you know which are the rarest birds in your country?

> *"You have to be a shady figure, increasing your visibility gradually."*

The database

All of the data is collated and put into a computerized database that can be accessed around the world. Some people working in the field log their own research onto computer systems. I love being in the field and getting to know the birds, but I also have to keep up to date with the research. While in Morocco, I had helpers back at the RSPB who helped with compiling and analyzing the data. The database is now managed by the National Park itself.

Protecting the area

Having the information on the Bald Ibis has already helped to prevent a European tourism company from building a massive resort here. We could prove that the resort would destroy an area where rare birds are found. It's tricky, because people here are poor and the resort would bring in money and create new jobs, but the birds would lose much of their ground. The threat from that company may have gone—it

Involving the locals

Many local people still survive through fishing and as shepherds and have a good working knowledge of the area, so they are ideal to train as wardens. Much of the training involves encouraging workers to focus more on the Ibis than they had been. International ornithologists watch the birds' progress with interest, but locals don't take much notice. The training is mostly on the job, with some group training sessions. This involved having to overcome language difficulties. I don't speak Arabic, which is the Moroccans' first language, and they don't speak English, so I had to rely on the French I learned as a schoolboy! My French has definitely gotten better, but, even so, we were communicating in a second or third language.

GARDIENS IN TRAINING
Ali (far left) and Chris trained wardens to make systematic records of data on birds in a way that is useful and reliable.

SOUSS-MASSA PARK
This National Park was created in 1991 to shelter the Bald Ibis colony nesting in the area. It is a long, slim strip of land stretching for 40 miles (65 km) along the Massa River between the towns of Agadir and Tiznit.

A tourist attraction

I lived near the park office with a Moroccan family on the edge of Agadir, which is a cosmopolitan and busy town. There is also a seaside resort nearby, so the area attracts tourists as well as birdwatchers. This part of the Moroccan coast is an important stopover for migrating birds enroute from the African sub-Sahara to breeding grounds in the Northern Hemisphere. It's also home to birds such as the Bald Ibis all year round.

Dying birds

While in Morocco, my conservation efforts took on more of an investigative role. Soon after I'd arrived in 1996, we suffered a huge setback—40 Ibises died in nine days. Out of the last 70 pairs of Bald Ibis more than a quarter died in just over a week. I was there to figure out how we could help the dwindling population. I felt helpless and very low and alone. There was very little anyone here could do to help.

Threats to the Ibis

We still don't really know what went wrong. We investigated the birds' corpses and ran tests for viruses and conditions we suspected could have killed them, but they were negative. We can't rule out West Nile Virus, but it's not clear. Before this disaster, the main threats the birds faced were changes to their habitat over the years, the use of restricted pesticides on crops by farmers in the region, and some hunting and fishing that disturbed their breeding.

Exciting news from Syria

There were once 50 colonies of these birds all over Morocco. That was around 100 years ago. Now all but one colony has gone, as have those in Algeria, Turkey, and, we thought, Syria. In 2002, though, an Italian researcher discovered three pairs breeding in Syria. He got in touch with me and I found out how the three pairs could be helped and sent suggestions. We have become good friends. A park has been set up there and the birds are now protected by local Bedouins and Syrian rangers.

Solving a mystery

Discovering the Syrian colony also presented a mystery, which involved international bird organizations. Unlike the colony in Morocco, which is nonmigratory and stays in the area all year round, no one knew where the Syrian birds went for the winter. Discovering where they wintered might tell us what problems the birds faced. Maybe hunting, overgrazing, or pesticides used in areas on the birds' migration route could be the cause of why

Ali monitors the birds with a telescope

"Trying to get the groups to work together toward the conservation of the species is our biggest challenge."

they were dying out. I went out to Syria to help to put satellite tags on the Ibises so we could track their migration routes. Getting permission for this from local authorities is not always easy, but eventually BirdLife partners in the Middle East helped to catch three of the four remaining adults. Once we got the tags on them, they were released and tracked by satellite, which was so exciting!

Investigating the birds' diet

It is strange the way things work out—I came to Morocco to study the Ibis and help save the last colony, and then these other pairs were discovered in Syria. Experts discovered a great deal about their habits, and finally learned that their winter home was Ethiopia. I was a little jealous, yes, but also so excited. We now get the data direct from the satellite tracking so we can see where the birds are and follow their journey.

Ground work

Back in Morocco, we had few facilities to speak of and not much support initially. As is often the case, trying to get the various groups—government officials, reserve workers, and bird protection agencies—to work together toward the conservation of a species is our biggest challenge. But we went in with a plan. It was clear that in order to preserve the Ibises, we needed to know what habitat they needed and what was happening to it.

Scientist at work

My work demands different skills. My knowledge of the Ibis is approaching that of a biologist, but I am a conservationist too. My research included examining a range of local beetles to match with the birds' faecal samples (or droppings) I had gathered, so I could identify the exact beetles the birds ate. The beetles are a very important part of the birds' diet—if the beetles can't survive locally, then this will affect the birds.

Living conditions

In many ways working in the field like this can be isolated and lonely with just me and a small Moroccan team. It was pretty tough for the first two years. I lived in Morocco for 9 months at a time, and gradually cut down, staying for 4 months and going off to other commitments in between. I rented a little place in a suburb of Agadir for a while, but I much preferred it when I moved into a home with a welcoming Moroccan family.

BIRDWATCHING
The reserve attracts birdwatchers and tourists from around the world—many come to see the Northern Bald Ibis. So the wardens have two roles—acting as knowledgeable guides, and protecting the birds and their habitat.

Birds and breeding

The breeding season is the most important time for monitoring the Northern Bald Ibis because we need to know whether they are rearing enough young to keep the population going, or whether some unknown problems might prevent this. Every day I'd note the contents of the nests—the the number of eggs and chicks. The first eggs appear in the last days of February and in March. They take a month to incubate and hatch. Finally, on about June 1st, the chicks follow the adults to the feeding grounds. The Northern Bald Ibis tend to stay put through the breeding season. After that, we monitor them three times a week, to check their numbers and what they are feeding on. The park wardens at Souss-Massa also collect data on vegetation, noting any changes. They note land use, things like the number of sheep grazing locally, and mark it all on maps.

Bald Ibis flock to roost at sunset

International group

We ended up creating an international advisory group of specialists involved with the Northern Bald Ibis, which I now chair. We discuss projects such as a reintroduction trial in Southern Spain, where Ibis bred in captivity are released into the wild. This involves vets, zoo and government officials, and researchers from that project, as well as other experts. It is rare to have such a diverse group,

but it's very good for sharing
information and working together.

The work continues

In between my field work I write
papers and articles for journals,
including an article called *Last
Chance for the Northern Bald Ibis*, to
draw attention to their plight. The
birds aren't totally safe yet, but they
are more secure. BirdLife is still
involved in Morocco but it's the wardens
who do the monitoring and recording now. Although
I am not close to the project any more, I've met the
staff at conferences, to help organize training, and I
still go back to see them each year.

Vultures in India

After leaving Souss-Massa, I went to India because
three species of vultures were dying out there and I
was needed to coordinate efforts to prevent total
extinction. The problem is that certain chemicals used

VULTURE CHICK
*Chris left Morocco in 2003 to head for
India, where three species of vulture
were in danger of dying out including
the White-rumped Vulture, seen here,
once one of the most common large
birds of prey in the world.*

to treat cattle are toxic to the
vultures, so we have had to
encourage the use of other less
harmful veterinary drugs. We also needed to get
funding for conservation breeding centers, to help
boost the number of birds and learn more about
them. There are now two breeding centres in India—
in West Bengal and Haryana—and my main role is to
support our Indian partner organization in these
efforts. It's not just about money, it's also about
changing people's habits. With bird protection, we are
trying to educate people and influence governments
to want to be involved in programs to save our rare
birds. As in Morocco, cooperation is the key!

Types of expert

TODAY, BIRD EXPERTS (ORNITHOLOGISTS) and amateur enthusiasts work together to study and protect birds and their habitats. They can work directly with animals in their environment, observe and record their behavior, or film their activities. Ornithologists have a range of different skills. They may be trained in conservation, biology, or even tourism and its impact.

FEEDING CONDORS WITH PUPPETS
One of the dangers of releasing captive birds into the wild is that they will have learned to identify with and depend on humans, and won't socialize properly with their own species. The California Condor chicks were fed with glove-puppet models of adult condors to keep them from "imprinting" on the humans looking after them.

THREATENED SPECIES BREEDER

Sometimes, experts are able to bring a species back from the brink of extinction. This was the case with the California Condor, one of the world's biggest vultures. The condor was once widespread throughout North America but, by the 1970s, just 30 birds remained. These last birds were taken into captivity for breeding. Some years later, researchers started releasing birds back into the wild. The program was a great success. There are now hundreds of condors and they are again breeding naturally.

TRAINING CRANES TO FLY
Whooping Cranes bred in captivity did not know how to migrate. Here, they are being taught the skill by following a microlite aircraft along their traditional migratory route, across the eastern United States.

TRACKER AND TAGGER

In Britain, the population of the Red Kite, a species of raptor, has increased hugely, thanks in part to tracking and tagging. By the mid 20th century British Red Kites had almost been wiped out through human persecution—loss of habitat, shooting for sport, and egg collecting. However, populations still flourished in other countries, and experts decided to try and reestablish the birds in Britain. Once there, the birds could be tracked by satellite and tagged to check that they remained in the country and bred successfully. During the early 1990s, 93 Red Kites from Sweden and Spain were released at two British sites. By 2006 there were almost 400 pairs of Red Kites in Britain, and it is the only country in which the Red Kite population is increasing.

TAGGING A RED KITE
Colored PVC tags are attached to the wings of a Red Kite at three / four weeks of age. The tags do not hinder the bird, and show when and where it was tagged and released.

NATURE FILMMAKER

In the past, observing animals in their natural habitats was the preserve of the dedicated specialist. Today, we can all see astonishing footage of creatures in their natural environment from our own homes. The assistance of ornithologists and other nature experts is invaluable in producing these films. They advise filmmakers on the best time of year to film and finding the right habitat. To get the right shot or sequence, patience is essential — camera operators may spend hours, days, or even weeks waiting for a rare bird to "display." They are aided by the latest technology — cameras so tiny that they can fit inside a bird's nest, night-vision cameras, ultra slow motion, and high-definition. The nature films of today provide important new information about animals' behavior, and may help conservationists understand how they might need help in the future.

FILMING FOR *THE BLUE PLANET*
A cameraman films penguins in the Antarctic for the BBC nature series, The Blue Planet. The eight-episode series took five years to make, involved filming in nearly 200 locations, and cost around $15 million. More than 12 million people watched it on its first transmission alone.

WILDLIFE ARTIST

Before the invention of photography and film, looking at sketches and paintings of birds was the only way most people could see birds from distant places. Accurate depictions were incredibly important. Artists such as François Martinet, Prideaux John Selby, and John Audobon, became famous among ornithologists for capturing the correct proportions, habits, and postures of birds. These artists often used specimens—dead stuffed birds—as models for their work. Today, we can identify bird species from photographs, but artists are still fascinated by the natural world. They continue to paint birds and other animals, live and on location in their own habitats.

"ARCTIC POOL"
Internationally acclaimed artist Bruce Pearson has been painting birds – here, Arctic Terns and Gray Phalaropes—for more than 30 years.

BIRDWATCHER

All over the world, millions of adults and children enjoy observing birds. All that is needed for the hobby is a pair of binoculars and a fair amount of patience. More serious birdwatchers may keep records of numbers of species seen, and can then contribute to local and national surveys of bird populations and migrations. Some observe birds from camouflaged shelters, called hides, so that they can study the birds close-up without disturbing them. Avid birdwatchers may make the activity a part of their vacation and travel.

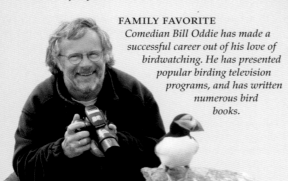

FAMILY FAVORITE
Comedian Bill Oddie has made a successful career out of his love of birdwatching. He has presented popular birding television programs, and has written numerous bird books.

CONSERVATIONIST

Sometimes, basic education can change practices that are killing huge numbers of birds. One campaign aims to save the albatross, threatened with extinction due to longline fishing. The birds get hooked and drowned on lines 30–62 miles (50–100 km) long. Albatrosses lay just one egg each year, and they are being killed faster than they can reproduce. The Albatross Task Force shows fishermen how to catch fish without endangering these and other seabirds. Some governments have also begun to impose restrictions on longline fishing.

SUMATRAN RAIN FOREST
Logging threatens three out of four bird species in Sumatra's lowland rain forest, including this Rufous-collared Kingfisher. The Royal Society for the Protection of Birds (RSPB) is working to help Indonesia protect the remaining forest.

FISHERIES ADVISOR
This fishing vessel is acting on the advice of the Albatross Task Force. It recommends fishing at night, when the birds are unlikely to be feeding, using bird-scarers such as lines with plastic streamers, weighting the line properly so that it sinks quickly out of birds' reach, and dyeing the bait blue, which puts birds off.

ECOTOUR SPECIALIST

Ecotourism tries to minimize the bad effects of tourism on local people and maximize the good effects. One of the good effects is employment, and ecotourism makes sure its jobs go to local people. In some remote places, the only work available might be logging—destroying large areas of forest and with it many animals' habitats. People desperate for ways to feed their families may even kill rare species to sell to illegal collectors. Ecotourism helps to provide them with alternative jobs and avoid damaging the environment. Tours led by local people are good for tourists too, because local people are likely to have all sorts of specialized knowledge, such as the best places to spot rare species.

GENERATING INCOME
These ecotourists and their guides keep their eyes peeled in Gambia's Baobalong Wetland Reserve. A responsible ecotour company will provide the training for local or indigenous people not only to become guides, but also to help manage the reserve.

Observing birds

BIRDS ARE VERY SENSITIVE to sound and movement, so humans observing them have to be as unobtrusive as possible. Cameras and radio transmitters are now so small that they can be fitted to birds' bodies, allowing humans to observe birds from far away and providing researchers with new information about their migratory patterns and other habits.

LO-TECH

Traditional methods of finding and observing birds are still vital for conservationists. By 1986, ornithologist Bharat Bhushan rediscovered a native bird of India, Jerdon's Courser, long thought to be extinct. His tools were little more than some modeling clay and a toy bird. He used the clay to catch the courser's footprints, and encouraged it to sing by playing mechanical bird calls. In Morocco and Syria, Bedouin nomads work with professionals to protect the breeding sites of the critically endangered Bald Ibis. When Moroccan nomads reported sightings of the birds in a perilous place, field workers used simple model birds to successfully lure the ibises to safe ledges, where they could nest.

Pencils for quick sketches

Binoculars

Sketch pad

Paint brush

Paints for accurate color

BASIC EQUIPMENT
A pair of binoculars is the essential tool of the birdwatcher. Many also make sketches of the birds they see. Drawing from life requires careful observation, so it is a good way of noting the important details that distinguish different species.

PHOTOGRAPHY
Some birdwatchers like to photograph the birds they see. A zoom lens makes the subject appear in close-up but can be heavy and may need to be held steadily on a tripod.

HI-TECH

New technology has helped researchers to solve some ornithological mysteries. Little was known about the migrating habits of Britain's Ospreys until the birds were tracked by satellite in 1999. Now, experts know how long the migrations take, what routes they use, and other information. Researchers have been able to pinpoint the wintering grounds of the Aquatic Warbler, Europe's most threatened migratory songbird. They caught some warblers at a nesting site and removed a few feathers. Warblers' feathers molt and new ones grow in the winter, on the wintering grounds. Detailed chemical analysis revealed exactly where the feathers had grown, and, therefore, where the birds wintered—a site just south of the Sahara Desert.

SKY DIVING WITH FALCONS
Spectacular footage may require spectacular methods. Working with a team of falconers, a skydiver has dived with Peregrine Falcons to record their speed of flight, and to film the birds of prey plummeting in their stoops, or dives. The Peregrine is the world's fastest bird, and can reach speeds of 300 km/h (186 mph) in a stoop.

Lightweight, solar-powered Eagle Cam attached by a temporary harness

HELICAM
A unique way of achieving aerial photography, a helicam is a tiny, remote-controlled helicopter fitted with a video camera. A helicam was used to produce footage of birds in flight for a television nature program.

EAGLE CAM
This specially adapted video camera has been used to make television footage and to keep tabs on a Golden Eagle called Bella that nests in Dublin, Ireland. Web-enabled Eagle Cams broadcast video footage of Bald Eagles interacting with their young on the internet.

Hall of fame

DURING THE LAST FEW CENTURIES many people have made major contributions to our knowledge and understanding of birds and their behavior. They include biologists, conservationists, artists, and broadcasters, as well as avid birdwatchers.

Sir David Attenborough on location with a hand-reared Golden Eagle

SALIM ALI

1896–1987

JOB: Ornithologist/naturalist
COUNTRY: India

Nicknamed the "Birdman of India," Salim Ali studied zoology at home and in Berlin, Germany. He went back to India and became one of the first to organize surveys of its bird populations. Determined to study birds in their natural habitat, Ali carried out most of his surveys in wild and remote places. He wrote several brilliant books about the birds of India and fought to save its important sites for birds, such as Keoladeo National Park.

SIR DAVID ATTENBOROUGH

1926–PRESENT

JOB: Broadcaster/naturalist
COUNTRY: UK

A world-famous broadcaster, Sir David Attenborough has written and hosted many television series covering almost every aspect of life on Earth. One of these series was *The Life of Birds* (1998), a study of the evolution and habits of birds all over the world. It took three years to make and involved filming trips to 42 countries. Sir David has probably done more than any other individual in the last 100 years to explain bird behavior to millions of people across the globe.

JOHN JAMES AUDUBON

1785–1851

JOB: Artist/writer
COUNTRY: US

Born on the Caribbean island of Haiti, Audubon grew up in boarding houses but went on to become one of the greatest bird artists in history. He moved to the US and set himself the task of painting and describing every kind of bird on the entire continent. When his vast *Birds of America* was finally published in several volumes from 1827 to 1838, it became an instant classic. Today, copies fetch several million dollars.

FLORENCE MERRIAM BAILEY

1863–1948

JOB: Environmentalist
COUNTRY: US

Bailey was outraged by the cruel slaughter of millions of egrets and other wild birds to provide feathers to decorate women's hats. Her campaign gathered momentum and eventually the trade was banned— one of the first great victories of the conservation movement in North America. Bailey was a passionate birdwatcher and gave inspiring speeches about her work.

THOMAS BEWICK

1753–1828

JOB: Wood engraver/ornithologist
COUNTRY: UK

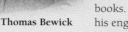

Thomas Bewick

As a child, Thomas Bewick showed an amazing talent for drawing, and at 14 he was sent to train as an engraver. He quickly became a partner in the firm. Bewick's beautiful, lifelike engravings were used to illustrate several best-selling books. To make his engravings, Bewick studied wild birds in the countryside so he could draw them accurately. This was very unusual at the time: most artists just used their imaginations instead. A type of swan—Bewick's Swan—is named in his honor.

SIR WALTER LAWRY BULLER

1838–1906

JOB: Lawyer/ornithologist

COUNTRY: New Zealand

Buller developed an interest in natural history, especially birds, as a child. He went on to write *A History of the Birds of New Zealand* (1872–73), and later published several updated versions. Buller's books reflect the 19th-century passion for shooting birds to display in private collections, which sadly involved the destruction of rare species.

Buller's Albatross

But he added a huge amount to our knowledge of New Zealand's bird life. In 1893, a species of albatross found in the South Pacific was named after him.

RACHEL CARSON

1907–64

JOB: Environmentalist

COUNTRY: US

Raised on a small family farm in Pennsylvania, Carson spent hours watching birds and exploring the natural world with her mother. During the 1940s and 1950s, she carried out brilliant research into the lethal effects of agricultural pesticides on birds and mammals. This led to her groundbreaking book, *Silent Spring* (1962), in which she described birds dying in their millions as a result of eating grain contaminated with pesticides. The book caused such a scandal that the pesticides were outlawed, and bird numbers began to recover.

HENRY EELES DRESSER

1838–1915

JOB: Entrepreneur/ornithologist

COUNTRY: UK

Dresser's great passion for birds started by collecting bird skins and eggs as a boy. A career in business took him all over Europe and to North America, and he always took the trouble to add to his collections on his travels. In the process, Dresser rapidly became one of the world's top ornithologists. His books include *A History of the Birds of Europe* (1871–81) and he also wrote more than 100 scientific articles on birds. Many articles described new species of bird, often from remote parts of the world, and they captivated his readers.

Starlings by Henry Dresser

JOHN GOULD

1804–81

JOB: Ornithologist

COUNTRY: UK

Gould became an expert at the art of taxidermy—preserving dead birds by stuffing them. By handling so many specimens he developed an amazingly detailed knowledge of bird anatomy and plumages. The famous naturalist Charles Darwin therefore decided to give Gould all the birds he had collected in the Galápagos Islands in the Pacific Ocean, so that he could identify them. Gould proved that some species were unique to the islands, and this played a crucial part in

Darwin's work. Gould later visited Australia with his wife Elizabeth, and together they published the first major illustrated guide to Australian birds in 1840–48.

ERNST HARTERT

1859–1933

JOB: Ornithologist

COUNTRY: Germany

A self-trained naturalist, Hartert became the curator of an ornithological museum in England in 1892. He traveled in India, Africa, and South America, gathering samples for the museum. When he finally retired in 1930, the museum held 280,000 specimens—the largest and most important private collection in the world. From this massive collection, Hartert described more than 1,000 of the species and subspecies.

Ernst Hartert

JANET KEAR

1933–2004

JOB: Ornithologist

COUNTRY: UK

In 1959, Kear joined the staff of the Wildfowl & Wetlands Trust (WWT), where she worked for the rest of her life. She was an expert on the world's wildfowl—a group of birds that includes swans, geese, and ducks. Kear had a major role in saving several rare species from extinction, including the Hawaiian Goose.

KONRAD LORENZ
1903–89
JOB: Zoologist
COUNTRY: Austria

Lorenz was one of the founders of ethology—the scientific study of animal behavior. As a child, he was given a one-day-old duckling and noticed how it followed him around as if he were its parent. This behavior is called imprinting, and Lorenz went on to study it in geese, becoming an expert on waterbirds. In 1973, together with Nikko Tinbergen (see page 25), he won a Nobel Prize for his discoveries about patterns of animal behavior.

Konrad Lorenz

CHRIS MEAD
1940–2003
JOB: Ornithologist
COUNTRY: UK

An expert on bird migration, Chris Mead worked for the British Trust for Ornithology (BTO) for more than 40 years. He was head of the Ringing Unit, which tags birds by attaching a numbered ring to them, so they can later be identified to find out about their migration, life span, and other aspects of their lives. In 2002, Mead trapped a Manx Shearwater (a species of seabird) that had originally been ringed in 1957 and calculated that it had flown around 5 million miles (8 million km) in its lifetime.

MARGARET MORSE NICE
1883–1974
JOB: Ornithologist
COUNTRY: US

Born in Massachusetts, Nice studied biology in college and became one of the most important women in the history of North American ornithology. During the 1920s, she carried out a detailed study of the birds of Oklahoma, a state which has huge areas of wide, open grassland and farmland. In 1927, she moved to Ohio and began a study of her local population of Song Sparrows. She carefully caught and ringed all of the sparrows in her research area so that she could identify each one, and then followed their changing fortunes. Over the years, Nice studied many generations of sparrows and gained a valuable insight into how populations of birds develop and change.

MAX NICHOLSON
1904–2003
JOB: Government minister/environmentalist
COUNTRY: UK

At the age of just 21, Nicholson had already made a career in ornithology with the publication of his first book about birds. Later, he held several high-flying jobs in the British government, while also campaigning to save the world's endangered species and unspoiled wild places. In 1961, Nicholson was part of the group that created the World Wide Fund for Nature (WWF). He was the chief editor of a huge multivolume book on the birds of Europe and North Africa.

ROGER TORY PETERSON
1908–96
JOB: Ornithologist/artist
COUNTRY: US

Peterson is famous as the inventor of modern bird identification guides. Previously, bird books had been awkward to use outdoors in the field, with poor illustrations and a complex layout. As a child, Peterson loved to sketch and identify birds, and his natural talent helped to turn his first book, *A Field Guide to Birds* (1934), into an overnight success. In this identification guide, similar types of bird were grouped on the same page to help comparison. Their important physical features were highlighted with arrows, making identification simple and clear.

PHOEBE SNETSINGER
1931–1999
JOB: Ornithologist
COUNTRY: US

When Snetsinger was diagnosed with life-threatening cancer in 1981, she decided to devote the rest of her time to seeing as many

Nikko Tinbergen paints chicken eggs during an experiment in camouflage

different kinds of bird as she could. Her quest took her to every corner of the world, from remote Arctic islands to tropical rain forests. She spent weeks planning each of her trips, which were funded by the fortune she had inherited from her father Leo Burnett, a wealthy businessman. In 1999, while on a birding trip to a remote region of Madagascar, off the coast of East Africa, she was killed instantly when her vehicle overturned. By the time of her death, she had managed to see over 8,500 species of bird—more than any other person in history.

Roger Tory Peterson with King Penguins

NIKKO TINBERGEN
1907–88
JOB: Zoologist
COUNTRY: Netherlands

Tinbergen was a lifelong friend and colleague of the zoologist Konrad Lorenz (see page 24). He shared a 1973 Nobel Prize with Lorenz for their discoveries about how groups of birds and other animals behave. He published several important books, including *The Herring Gull's World* (1953). In it, he examined the way in which young gulls automatically peck at the bright red spot on their parent's bill to stimulate the adult to feed them.

GILBERT WHITE
1720–93
JOB: Priest/naturalist
COUNTRY: UK

White earned his living as a priest and lived in a number of vicarages in southern England. However, he is best known for his observations and writings about the natural world, some of which he collected in his book *The Natural History and Antiquities of Selborne* (1789). This masterpiece is still read and quoted from today. White believed in distinguishing birds by painstaking observation instead of collecting specimens with a shotgun, like most other naturalists of his time. He was one of the first people to separate the very similar-looking Willow Warbler, Chiffchaff, and Wood Warbler. He recognized that they must be three different species because their songs were totally different. Among other topics, he wrote about bird migration, but he never solved the mystery of where Swallows disappeared to in winter.

FRANCIS WILLUGHBY
1635–72
JOB: Naturalist
COUNTRY: UK

In 1662, Willughby and fellow naturalist John Ray began to collect material for a book. They studied breeding seabirds on the west coast of England, then made

Alexander Wilson

further studies in the Netherlands, Germany, Switzerland, and Italy. Unfortunately, Willughby died before their results were published as the *Ornithologia Libri Tres* in 1676. The book revolutionized the way in which birds were classified by organizing species according to their physical characteristics.

ALEXANDER WILSON
1766–1813
JOB: Ornithologist/illustrator
COUNTRY: UK

Wilson was born into a poor family, and spent his early adult life as a weaver. In 1794, he immigrated to North America, hoping for a better life. He became interested in ornithology, and resolved to produce a book showing all the North American birds. Wilson traveled all around the country, observing and painting birds. His nine-volume *American Ornithology* was published between 1808 and 1814, illustrating 268 species of birds, 26 of which had never been described before.

2

ACTIVITIES

Have you got what it takes to be an ornithologist? Find out how much you know and hone your skills with our challenging activities.

Which expert are you?

Inspired by the stories of the experts in your pack, you've decided you would like to work with birds. But there are so many fascinating areas to go into—which will you choose? Use this fun flowchart to help you out!

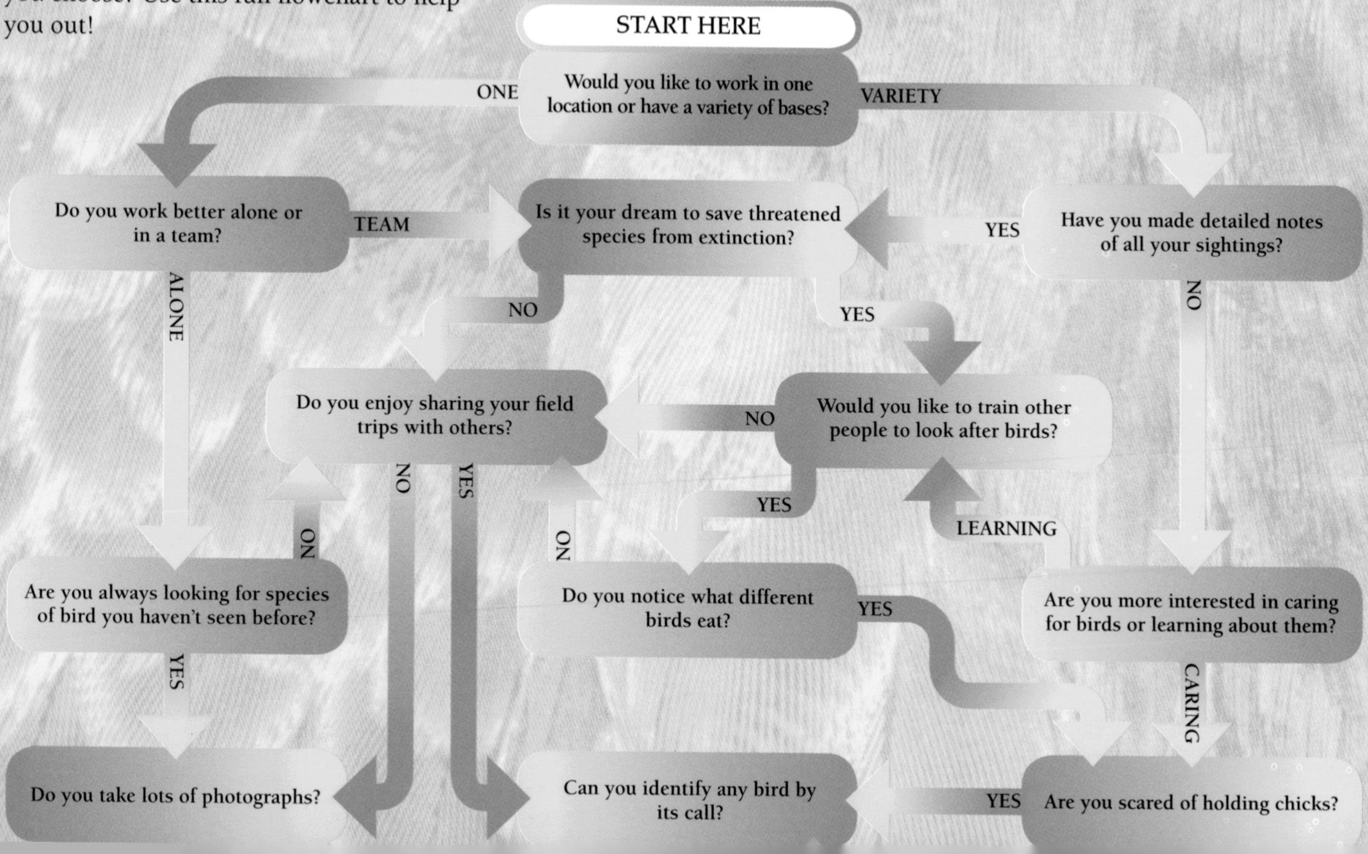

START HERE

Would you like to work in one location or have a variety of bases?

VARIETY

Have you made detailed notes of all your sightings?

NO

Are you more interested in caring for birds or learning about them?

CARING

Are you scared of holding chicks?

YES

LEARNING

Would you like to train other people to look after birds?

YES

YES

Is it your dream to save threatened species from extinction?

YES

NO

NO

Do you notice what different birds eat?

Can you identify any bird by its call?

ONE

Do you work better alone or in a team?

TEAM

Do you enjoy sharing your field trips with others?

YES

NO

ON

ALONE

Are you always looking for species of bird you haven't seen before?

YES

Do you take lots of photographs?

Would you like to bring the world new information about birds?

YES → Would you enjoy using scientific equipment?

NO → Do you like to travel to different countries?

ON → Do you have a gentle, caring nature?

YES → Would you become attached to birds you reared by hand?

YES

YES

DON'T MIND

NO

NO → Would you be happy showing visitors around?

YES → Do you prefer to get involved in nature or simply observe?

INVOLVED

OBSERVE

NO

YES

BREEDER

Your gentle nature would allow you to care for young birds without them becoming dependent on you. You may even help bring a species back from the brink of extinction!

NATURE FILMMAKER

You are happiest observing animals in their natural habitat and would relish the chance to bring amazing images to the public that they would never get to see without you.

RESERVE MANAGER

Protecting birds in their natural habitats is very important to you. You dream of an environment where wildlife can flourish and live in harmony with humans.

ORNITHOLOGIST

You are driven to find out everything you can about birds. Luckily, you have the mind of a biologist and the technical know-how to succeed!

Beak match

Most birds grasp their food with their beaks. The shape is very important because it allows them to tackle certain types of food. Can you check the food that each beak is best adapted for?

HOW LONG
DID IT TAKE YOU?

☐ 10 mins:
Expert

☐ 15 mins:
Knowledgeable

☐ 20 mins:
Beginner

🔍 Look out! There might be more than one answer for some questions.

A. Capercaillie

Seeds ☐

Needles of conifer trees ☐

Strips of meat and fur ☐

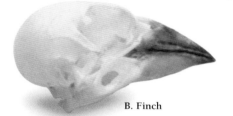

B. Finch

C. Woodpecker

Hard-cased seeds ☐   Insects ☐   Seafood ☐

Beetle larvae ☐   Fish ☐   Worms ☐

ACTIVITY—MAKE BAGEL BIRD FEEDERS

Cut a bagel in half. Spread peanut butter on the two flat sides and sprinkle bird seed on top. Pat down the seeds. Refrigerate the bagel halves for ten minutes so the seeds stick to the peanut butter. Remove from the fridge and tie a piece of string to each half so they can hang from a tree. Hang your bird feeders up and wait, from a distance, for the birds to arrive. Make a note of any you recognize!

D. Avocet

E. Owl

Ribbon worms   Hard-cased seeds   Grass

☐   ☐   ☐

Strips of meat   Fish   Seeds from fields
and fur

☐   ☐   ☐

Pellets

Predatory birds swallow their food whole, including the fur, feathers, and bones. Because they cannot digest these pieces, they regurgitate them as pellets. Look closely at these pellets. Which birds do they come from?

Do you need some help? Check out *Eyewitness Bird.*

1..

2..

3..   4..   5..

Bird groups

One way of classifying birds is to group them in terms of similar characteristics or habitats. Which groups do you think these birds belong to? Look at the list of bird groups, then put a number in each box.

BIRD GROUPS

1. Gamebirds
2. Parrots
3. Flightless birds
4. Birds of prey
5. Herons/storks
6. Waterbirds
7. Seabirds
8. Shorebirds
9. Tropical birds
10. Songbirds
11. Near passerines

Laughing
Kookaburra ☐

Blue-crowned
Trogon ☐

Sulfur-crested
Cockatoo ☐

Scarlet Ibis ☐

Brown Pelican ☐

Scarlet-chested
Sunbird ☐

Marabou Stork ☐

🔍 Use the profile
cards to check
your answers.

Himalayan Monal

Brown Kiwi

Mute Swan

Bald Eagle

Take flight

Now work out whether these birds are migrants, partial migrants, or nonmigrants.

M	P	NM
Migrant	Partial	Nonmigratory

Brown Kiwi

Blue-crowned Trogon

Marabou Stork

Scarlet Ibis

Bald Eagle

Brown Pelican

Scarlet-chested Sunbird

Sulfur-crested Cockatoo

Laughing Kookaburra

Mute Swan

Himalayan Monal

Use the profile cards to make this exercise a soaring success.

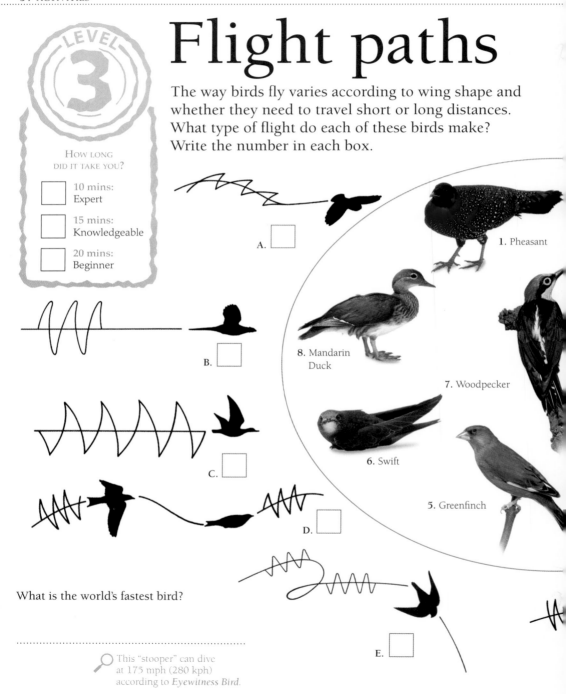

Flight paths

The way birds fly varies according to wing shape and whether they need to travel short or long distances. What type of flight do each of these birds make? Write the number in each box.

LEVEL 3

How long did it take you?

☐ 10 mins: Expert

☐ 15 mins: Knowledgeable

☐ 20 mins: Beginner

A. ☐

B. ☐

C. ☐

D. ☐

E. ☐

1. Pheasant

8. Mandarin Duck

7. Woodpecker

6. Swift

5. Greenfinch

What is the world's fastest bird?

....

🔍 This "stooper" can dive at 175 mph (280 kph) according to *Eyewitness Bird*.

H.

G.

2. Peregrine Falcon

3. Roller

4. Barn Owl

F.

Wing it

Complete these sentences by filling in the name of the bird that fits the flight description.

1. ....
shuts its wings periodically to save energy.

2. ....
climbs and dives much more steeply than most other birds.

3. ....
has a slow, buoyant flight.

4. ....
alternates fast wingbeats with short glides.

5. ....
has rapid wingbeats followed by a long glide.

6. ....
has a heavy up and down flight.

7. ....
dives with its wings partially folded.

8. ....
beats its wings constantly during flight.

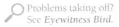 Problems taking off?
See *Eyewitness Bird.*

LEVEL

3

HOW LONG
DID IT TAKE YOU?

☐ 10 mins:
Expert

☐ 15 mins:
Knowledgeable

☐ 20 mins:
Beginner

Eggstravaganza

Bird eggs come in all shapes, sizes, colors, and numbers,
depending on the type of bird and its habitat. Do you
recognize any of these eggs? Put a letter in each box to
match the egg to the bird.

Which bird lays the biggest
egg of any bird alive today?
See *Eyewitness Bird* for
eggstra help!

A. Moorhen

C. Nightingale

B. Ostrich

D. Emu

G. Albatross

It is illegal to disturb nesting
birds or bird eggs.

E. Grebe

F. Heron

1.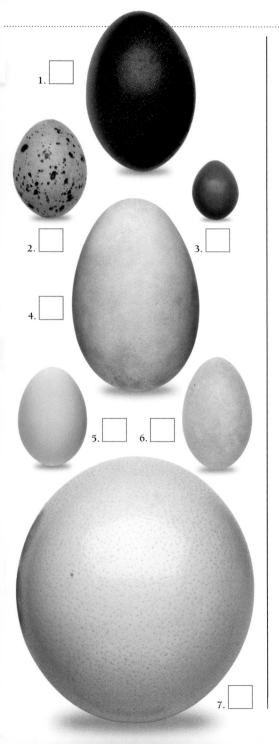

2.

3.

4.

5. 6.

7.

Nests

What are these nests made out of? Draw a line joining each nest to the material it is made from. Then write down which bird the nests belong to.

A. Moss and lichen

1...

B. Leaves and grass

2...

C. Feathers

3...

D. Mud

4...

E. Hair

5...

Body double

What makes a bird a bird? By looking at its body parts, inside and out, we can identify the characteristics that these animals share. Test your knowledge by labeling the pictures, then use *Eyewitness Bird* to check your answers.

HOW LONG
DID IT TAKE YOU?

☐ 10 mins:
Expert

☐ 15 mins:
Knowledgeable

☐ 20 mins:
Beginner

A...............................

S................................

B...........................

R...........................

C.................

....

Q.............................

D...................

P.............................

E.......................

O.............................

F...............................

N...............................

G...............................

M...............................

H ....

K...............................

I...............................

L...............................

J...............................

Look for another feathered friend in *Eyewitness Bird* for help.

Chaffinch outer surface

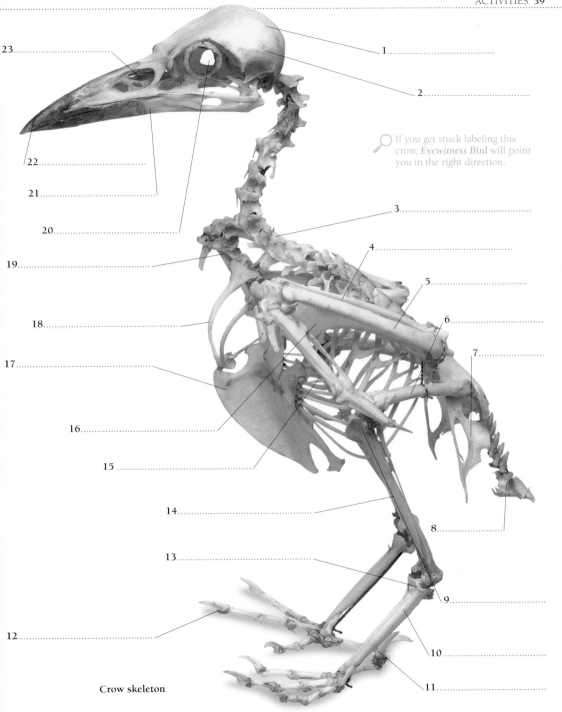

23.....

1.....

2.....

If you get stuck labeling this crow, *Eyewitness Bird* will point you in the right direction.

22.....

21.....

20.....

19.....

18.....

17.....

16.....

15 .....

14.....

13.....

12.....

3.....

4.....

5.....

6.....

7.....

8.....

9.....

10.....

11.....

Crow skeleton

③

EXPERTS' LOG

It's time to get organized and start your
own research. Check out the simple tools
that every budding expert needs. Your career
in ornithology starts here!

In the field

Tools
- Notebook
- Pen
- Camera
- Binoculars
- Colored pencils
- Plastic bags to store feathers

• Train your eye to recognize a bird's key features by keeping a notebook or log where you can sketch and note its behavior. Binoculars help you to see the details, but don't worry if you don't have a pair—you can still see a lot by just looking.

• Record your sightings in detail. Include where you spotted each bird, what time of day and year it was, a short description of its appearance, call, and behavior, and its name, if you can identify it.

• Drawing is more fun than writing extensive notes! Don't worry if you're not a great artist; sketching details such as beaks, feathers, or feet with colored pencils will still help to build up your knowledge.

• Watch how your bird flies and use the simple silhouette drawings on page 29 to help you describe it.

• Look for loose feathers on the ground and try to find out which part of the body and which bird they come from.

• Be careful not to disturb birds when you are watching them. This is particularly important for parent birds with nests and young—always keep your distance.

Becoming a bird expert requires lots of patience and careful observation. You'll be amazed at how many species live near you, so get watching!

At the museum

Tools
• Pen
• Notebook
• Camera

• Many natural history museums display a fascinating range of preserved specimens from common birds such as blackbirds to rare and even extinct species.

• One of the world's most impressive exhibits is a cast of a rare fossil of *Archaeopteryx*, thought to be the link between birds and dinosaurs. It is on show at London's Natural History Museum. See page 68 of *Eyewitness Bird* for other places to visit.

• Some nature reserves and seabird centers film their wildlife. You can view the images on a screen in the visitor center and zoom into the smallest details without disturbing the birds.

• Take notes from information cards that accompany your favorite exhibits. Be as detailed as you can about what the bird looks like, where it lives, and its behavior. Use the space here for notes, or start your own log in a notebook or scrapbook.

• If the museum or reserve allows you to take photographs, attach them here to help you remember your trip. If not, visit their gift shop to look for postcards of your favorite birds and add these to your scrapbook.

If exotic and rare birds are unlikely to visit your yard or local park, the best place to learn more about them is a museum or wildlife center.

Research

TOP TIPS

Books
An essential resource for any expert!
Visit your local library or bookshop to
look up information about a bird you
have observed in the field or for clues
about where you can expect a sighting
of your favorite species.

The newspapers
Watch out for reports of rare sightings
or conservation projects in the news.
You may like to start a separate file for
newspaper clippings, or attach them
here. Use the map in your Expert
pack for marking up the locations and
details of interesting sightings as you
hear about them. If the species isn't in
your Profile Cards, make a new card
to add to your collection.

The web
Get online to find information about
birds all around the world, including
top birdwatching hot spots. The RSPB
and BirdLife have informative sites
where you can also look for local
events and groups that you could join.
Check out the listings on page 69 of
Eyewitness Bird.

Museums and wildlife centers
Contact your nearest natural history
museum or reserve and find out if
they have an exhibition or interesting
birds for you to visit.

An expert's knowledge is based on a lot of patient
research as well as observation. So make this an
important part of your study, too.

Scrapbook

Attach your sketches and photographs in this space together with any postcards you have bought. Have a go at drawing an exotic bird that you would love to see!

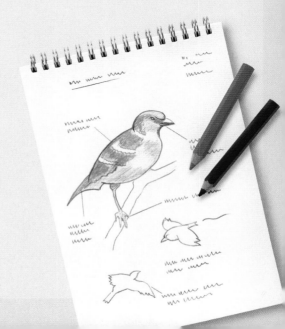

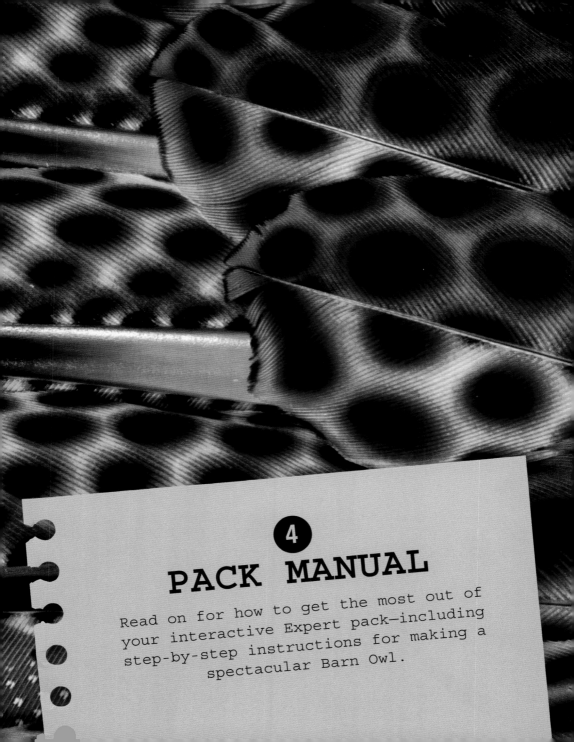

4

PACK MANUAL

Read on for how to get the most out of your interactive Expert pack—including step-by-step instructions for making a spectacular Barn Owl.

Expert reads

Everything you need to know about getting the most from your interactive Expert pack is right here! Written by the experts of today for the experts of tomorrow, these reads will speed you on your journey to uncovering the wonders of ornithology. Read on!

Eyewitness Guide

Your first port of call for all things feathered, this museum on a page is where you can be an eyewitness to the fascinating world of birds. Written by experts and illustrated with incredible photographs of nature close-up, *Eyewitness Bird* is an essential read for every budding expert.

Wallchart

How do feathers work? What did birds evolve from? Put this chart on your wall at home or at school and the answers to your bird questions will never be far away.

48 BLUE BIRD
Paradisaea rudolphi

JUVENILE

FIELD
The
out
vib
a
s

Feathers

THE FEATHERS that make up a bird's plumage are of four main types—down feathers, body feathers and the feathers of the tail and wings. Although many of them are drab and unremarkable, others are beautifully shaped and colored structures.

BODY FEATHERS
The feathers that streamline a bird's body

DOWN FEATHERS
Soft, finely divided feathers layer of air to provide insul

Parrots

African gray parrot

Macaw

Macaws

Red lory

Pigeon

TAIL FEATHERS
Feathers for steering, balance, and display.

Goose

Flamingo

Peacock

TAIL FEATHERS
A bird uses its tail feathers to steer when in flight and to balance when perched or on the ground. Some male birds, such as pheasants, have especially long or brightly colored tail feathers. These play an important part in courtship, to help the male attract a mate.

Bird features

Birds have lightweight skeletons and fewer bones than reptiles or mammals. Many of a bird's larger bones are hollow, to aid flight. Most birds have excellent vision, which helps them spo their prey and avoid their enemies.

Har
f

Wing feathers

Upper tail feathers

Tail fea

Gull

Macaw

On the w

Only a few ar bats, and bird of powered f three, birds and most p mainly bec of their wi strong, lig It is also s front to b pull the flaps th Althou

OUTER WING FEATHERS
Outer wing feathers, the strongest feathers in a bird's plumage, provide most of the power for flight. The outermost feathers

Profile Cards

Pull out these handy pocket-size cards and bone up on the essential facts that every expert should know. Use them to test your friends' knowledge, too, or make some of your own to add to your collection!

38 TOCO TOUCAN

Ramphastos toco

bare yellow skin around eye

large hollow beak

FIELD NOTES

With an enormous hollow, light beak, this to to reach food on the ends of thin twigs, whi be too heavy to perch on. It feeds mainly or insects. It moves around with big boundin utters a deep, croaking call.

FACT FILE

LENGTH: 24 in (60 cm)	WINGS
GROUP: Tropical	POPU
NUMBER OF EGGS: 3–4	LIFE SPAN: 20 ye
HABITAT: Woodland	MIGRATION: Nonmigrant
LIVES: Northeast and Central South America	

32 KAKAPO

Strigops habroptilus

CR

mottled camouflage plumage

stout build

FIELD NOTES

This parrot is a nocturnal bird and lives on the ground, roosting in trees by day and feeding on flowers, fruit, and seeds at night. It is unable to fly, but can glide downhill. It was threatened with extinction by the introduction of rats and stoats but survives on predator-free islands.

FACT FILE

LENGTH: 25 in (63 cm)	
GROUP: Parrot	
NUMBER OF EGGS: 1–3	WINGSPAN: 3 ft 9 in (1.2 m)
HABITAT: Trees/bushes	POPULATION: 50
LIVES: New Zealand	LIFE SPAN: 60 years
	MIGRATION: Nonmigrant

FINCH FLIGHT
Finches have bro rounded wings, shut periodicall to save energy.

TURTLE DOV
Doves and pi their wings r pauses, to he from predat

SWALLOW
A swallow's wings ena continuou wingbeat

OWL
The ow soft, fri its wir hunt i

BUZ
Hea such the risi

PI
W
p

DK EYEWITNESS WALL CHARTS

BIRD

THERE ARE OVER 9,500 SPECIES OF BIRD and they live in a huge range of habitats, from deserts and tropical rain forests to the polar ice caps. Birds have wings covered with feathers, enabling them to fly. Some birds fly on long journeys, called migrations, to breed or to find food. All birds reproduce by laying eggs, and many build nests to rear their young.

Dinosaur to bird

The fossilized remains of *Archaeopteryx*, a creature with feathers, clawed wings, and tiny pointed teeth, provides evidence that birds probably evolved from dinosaurs over 150 million years ago.

Breast feathers

covered h scales

Alula feathers held open in slow flight to prevent stalling

n g is

om s to

Outer wing feathers help bird to steer when in flight

Small covert feathers shape the wing's leading edge (the part that meets the oncoming air)

Main covert feathers arranged in rows along the inner and outer wing

INNER WING FEATHER

Mapping migration

The migration routes of birds crisscross almost every corner of the planet. Bird migration used to be a mystery but today it is studied in many ways, and this research provides valuable data to help bird conservation. One survey method is bird ringing or tagging. As more and more birds are monitored, scientists gradually build up a picture about their breeding and wintering grounds and the incredible journeys they make.

Tagging Whooper Swans
This research team is attaching a satellite tag to a Whooper Swan on its remote breeding ground in Mongolia. The tag's miniature transmitter is solar-powered and uses global positioning system (GPS) technology to send data via satellite back to the team's computers. In this way the scientists always know where the swan is. After a few years, the tag's strap degrades and falls off, leaving the bird unharmed.

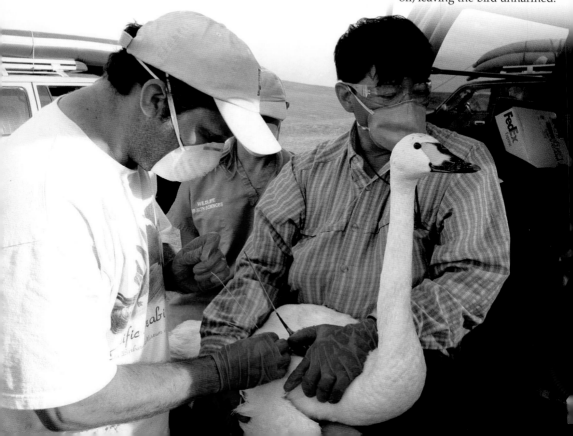

Your map

Over the past 150 years, the world's bird experts have uncovered a huge amount of information about the seasonal comings and goings of migratory birds. Some of these people were professional scientists working for governments or charities, but others were ordinary birdwatchers who simply enjoyed studying birds as a hobby. Together, this army of dedicated people has transformed our knowledge of bird behavior, using techniques as varied as bird ringing, satellite tagging, and patient observation in the wild. The fold-out map in your pack features many of their fascinating discoveries and reveals some of the extraordinary long-distance journeys that birds make.

Whooper Swan migration

This computer-generated map was plotted from the data sent back by four Whooper Swans in the fall of 2006. The location of each bird was recorded every two hours and stored in its transmitter's memory, before being sent by email to the research team's waiting computer. On this map, the route taken by each bird is shown in a different color, together with the date at each location.

Eyewitness **Bird** Map

Incredible journeys

THE ANNUAL MIGRATION of billions of birds is one of the greatest wonders of the natural world and has fascinated people since ancient times. Many migratory birds, or migrants, travel vast distances across oceans or continents to reach their destinations, often flying nonstop for hours. Other migrants move only a few miles, up or down a mountain, or to the nearest coast, for instance. Different species of bird set off at different times and travel at different speeds, some by day and others at night. This map shows a few of their most amazing journeys.

ARCTIC TERN

This elegant seabird flies across the world and back every year—the longest annual migration of any bird. It travels between its breeding grounds in the Arctic and its wintering grounds on the edge of the Antarctic pack ice and then back again—a round trip of up to 25,000 miles (40,000 km).

This swan nests in Siberia. The swan head to northwest from eastern Sib and Japan. Fam young birds ca

NORTH AMERICA

Arctic Circle

PACIFIC OCEAN

Tropic of Cancer

ROCKHOPPER PENGUIN ROUTE

Falkland Islands

Scale
0 km 100   200   300   400
0 miles   100   200   300

Seabirds are difficult to track while far from land. To discover where Rockhopper Penguins catch their fish, researchers on the Falkland Islands fitted some nesting birds with backpacks containing miniature satellite transmitters. These showed that the penguins headed out to sea by swimming counterclockwise around the islands, and followed the ocean currents to reach the best fishing grounds. Each fishing trip lasted 16–27 days, during which the penguin traveled an average of 250 miles (400 km).

Key — Migratory birds

Distribution   Migra

Arctic Tern

Bewick's Swan

Blackpoll Warble

Bobolink

Eastern Red-footed

Franklin's G

Red Kno

Manx Shear

Pied Flyca

Red-footed

Scarlet Ta

Swainson

White

Yellow

Scale (at equator)
0 km   2,000
0 miles

FLYWAYS

MANX SHEAR

Multimedia

Handing in school projects has never been so exciting! Packed with specialized images and facts about birds, this clip-art CD will make your homework look so professional you'll be dying to show it off. Go to www.ew.dk.com for more interactive, downloadable information.

Clip-art CD

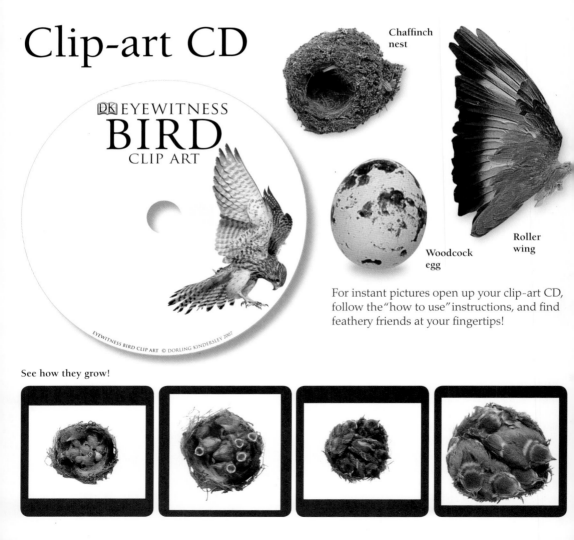

Chaffinch nest

Woodcock egg

Roller wing

DK EYEWITNESS
BIRD
CLIP ART

EYEWITNESS BIRD CLIP ART © DORLING KINDERSLEY 2007

For instant pictures open up your clip-art CD, follow the "how to use" instructions, and find feathery friends at your fingertips!

See how they grow!

Model owl

Build on your own expert knowledge of bird anatomy by assembling these pieces to make a model Barn Owl. You'll find step-by-step instructions on the next page.

You'll find step-by-step instructions on the next page.

Before you start assembling the boxes, press out the pieces and fold the cardboard along the score lines. White areas on tabs indicate where pieces should be glued together.

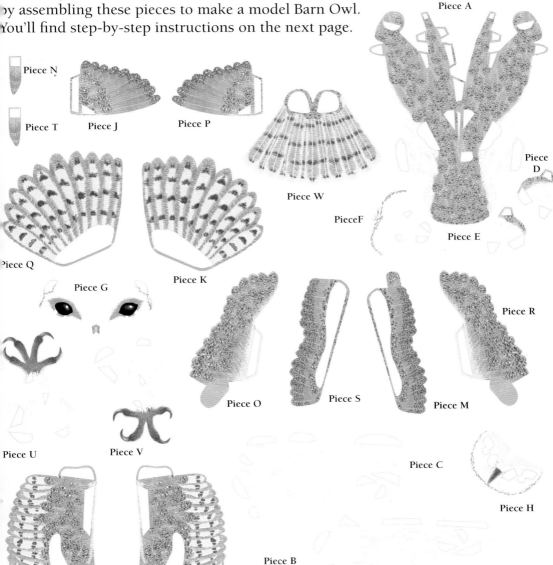

Piece A

Piece N

Piece T

Piece J

Piece P

Piece W

Piece F

Piece D

Piece E

Piece Q

Piece G

Piece K

Piece R

Piece O

Piece S

Piece M

Piece U

Piece V

Piece C

Piece H

Piece I

Piece L

Piece B

ASSEMBLING THE BODY SECTION

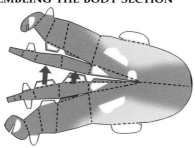

1 On piece A, glue tabs 1, 2, 3, and 4 to the reverse side, where labeled.

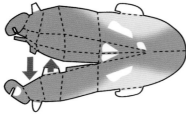

2 Slide tabs 5 and 6 under the cardboard and glue onto the reverse side, where indicated. Repeat with tabs 7 and 8.

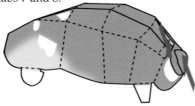

3 Slot the two sides of head piece 9 and 10 together, apply glue and secure. Ensure that the two middle tabs are tucked behind.

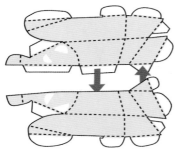

4 Press out the two chest pieces B and C, attach them together with tabs 11 and 12.

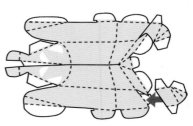

5 Glue pieces D and E onto tabs 13 and 14. Glue tabs 15 and 16 to the underside of the chest piece, where marked.

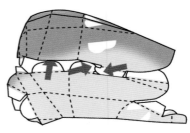

6 Attach piece A to the chest section by slotting and gluing tabs 17 and 18 together and sticking tab 19 onto the inside, where marked. Repeat step 6 on the other side with tabs 20, 21, and 22.

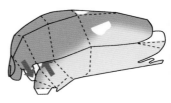

7 Glue the side tabs—23, 24, 25, and 26—of pieces D and E under the head, onto the areas indicated.

MAKING THE FACE

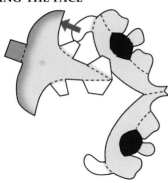

1 Glue tab 27 on eye piece G, behind the top head piece F, where marked.

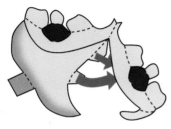

2 Pushing and curving the eye piece into the curve of piece F, glue tabs 28 and 29 in position. Fold the side of G around and continue gluing tabs 30, 31, and 32 in position.

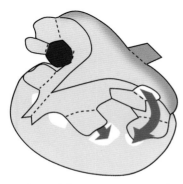

3 Glue tab 33 of the eye section onto face piece H, where marked. Bending the eye section, glue tabs 34 and 35 into position. You will need to squeeze the front section to glue down tabs 36, 37, and 38.

ATTACHING THE FACE TO THE BODY

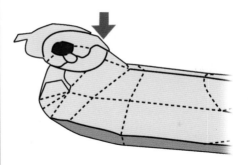

1 Glue the bottom of the assembled head onto tab 39 on the body.

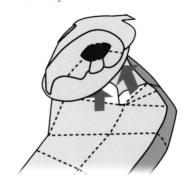

2 Apply glue to body tabs 40, 41, 42, and 43. Push the head against these tabs, pressing to secure in place.

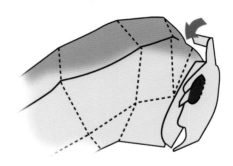

3 Glue and fold top face tab 44 behind slotted pieces 9 and 10 and secure.

MAKING THE WINGS

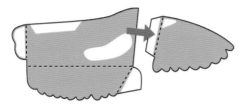

1 Join pieces I and J together by gluing tab 45a in position.

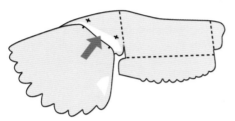

2 Turn the piece over and glue piece K in place, (matching pinholes and notches together).

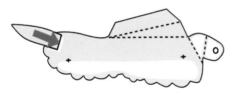

3 Glue piece N onto the underside of piece O, as marked.

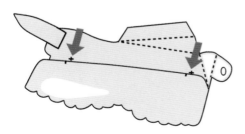

4 Glue pieces M and O together, (matching pinholes and notches together as before).

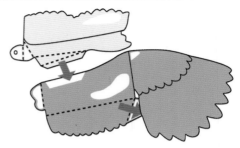

5 Glue tab 49a in position, then bend the wing and glue tab 50a under the long feathers piece.

6 Turn the top section over and, pushing forward so that the front edge is vertical, glue tabs 51a and 52a down. Repeat all the moves with the other wing.

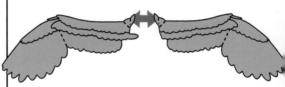

7 Join both wings by gluing tabs 53a and 53b together.

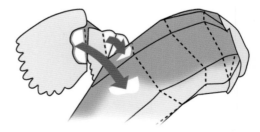

8 Attach the wings to the body, glue tab 54 in place, bend the wings over the body and glue tabs 55, 56, and 57. Glue small tab 58 in place on the back of the owl.

ASSEMBLING THE LEGS

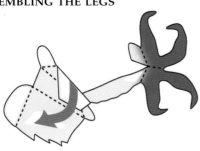

FINISHING THE MODEL

1 On piece U, fold the top side over and attach tab 59a in place.

1 On tail piece W, glue tabs 66 and 67 inside the body piece, where indicated.

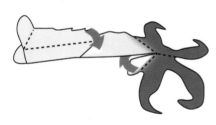

2 Fold the leg against tab 60a and glue, then fold tab 61a of the foot behind the leg and secure. Repeat with the other leg.

2 Push tabs 68, 69, and 70 under the cardboard edges and secure to the marked areas. Apply glue to tabs 71,72,73, and 74, tuck tabs 71 and 72 inside the body area and press tabs 73 and 74 down on the white areas on the tail piece. Press the back of the model against the inside tabs to secure.

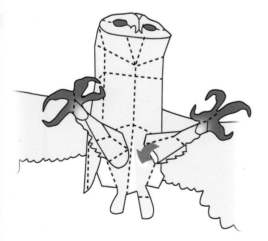

hang owl from tab on back with string.

3 Glue the legs onto the body, as indicated by the marked white areas.

Index

Activity answers

Page 30–31 Beak match
A. Capercailie, seeds and needles of conifer trees.
B. Finch, hard-cased seeds.
C. Woodpecker, beetle larvae.
D. Avocet, ribbon worms.
E. Owl, strips of meat. Fur is swallowed and discarded as pellets.

Pellets
1. Wader.
2. Crow.
3. Songbird.
4. Falcon.
5. Little owl.

Page 32–33 Bird groups & Take flight
Himalayan Monal, 1, NM.
Sulfur-crested Cockatoo, 2, NM.
Brown Kiwi, 3, NM.
Bald Eagle, 4, P.
Marabou Stork, 5, NM.
Mute Swan, 6, NM.
Brown Pelican, 7, M.
Scarlet Ibis, 8, NM.
Blue-crowned Trogon, 9, NM.
Scarlet-chested Sunbird, 10, NM.
Laughing Kookaburra, 11, NM.

Page 34–35 Flight paths
A. 4; B. 1; C. 8; D. 3; E. 2; F. 7; G. 5; H. 6.

Wing it
1. The Greenfinch.
2. The Woodpecker.
3. The Barn Owl.
4. The Swift.
5. The Pheasant.
6. The Roller.
7. The Peregrine Falcon.
8. The Mandarin Duck.

The world's fastest bird is the Peregrine Falcon.

Page 36–37 Eggstravaganza
A. 2.
B. 7.
C. 3.
D. 1.
E. 5.
F. 6.
G. 4.

Nests
A.—5.—Chaffinch.
B.—1.—Nightingale.

C.—3.—Redstart.
D.—4.—Songthrush.
E.—2.—Reed Bunting.

Page 38–39 Body double
Chaffinch
A. Eye; B. Nostril; C. Upper mandible of beak; D. Lower mandible of beak; E. Breast; F. Alula; G. Wing coverts; H. Flank; I. Toe; J. Tarsus; K. Under-tail coverts; L. Tail; M. Upper-tail coverts; N. Rump; O. Primary flight feathers; P. Secondary flight feathers; Q. Mantle; R. Nape; S. Ear.

Crow
1. Cranium; 2. Ear; 3. Backbone; 4. Radius; 5. Ulna; 6. Femur; 7. Hip girdle; 8. Pygostyl or pelvis; 9. Knee joint; 10. Tarsus; 11. Hind toe; 12. Claw; 13. Ankle; 14. Tibia; 15. Metacarpus; 16. Humerus; 17. Keel; 18. Wishbone; 19. Coracoid bone; 20. Eye socket; 21. Lower mandible of beak; 22. Upper mandible of beak; 23. Nostril.

Acknowledgments

The publisher would like to thank the following for their kind permission to reproduce their photographs:

(Key: a-above; b-below/bottom; bl-below/bottom right; br-below/bottom right; c-center; cl-center left; cr-center right; cra-center right above; crb-center right below; l-left; r-right; t-top; tl-top left; tr-top right.)

Expert Files
Adventure Archive: 21tr; **Alamy Images**: Val Duncan/Kenebec Images 2-3; Gôran Heckler/pixonnet.com 40-41; ImageState/ Tom Walker 26-27; Dave Watts 8-9r; **The Art Archive**: 23tc; **Corbis**: 16t; Bettmann 24t; Vasily Fedosenko/Reuters 29b; Darrell Gulin 50-51; Peter Johnson 25bl; **FLPA**: Tui De Roy/Minden Pictures 23cl; **Getty Images**: Nina Leen/Time & Life Pictures 24br; **Farah Ishtiaq-Bowden** 8t; **Lonely Planet Images**: Andrew Burke 18-19bc; **Mary Evans Picture Library**: 22b;

25tr; **naturepl.com**: 29ca; Doug Allan 17b; Nigel Bean 18bl; John Downer 21b; Tony Heald 29cb; Tom Hugh-Jones 16b; William Osborn 36br; Jason Venus 21cl; **OSF**: 32tr; Bruce Pearson: 18t; **Photoshot/NHPA**: Bill Coster 1fclb; **Rex Features**: Nature Picture Library 22tr; **RSPB**: BirdLife International 19tr; Chris Bowden 8bl, 10tr, 11t, 11b, 12bl, 14-15t; Chris Gomershall 10tl, 13t, 13b; Jacob Wijpkema 19cl; **rspb-images.com**: Chris Gomersall 14b, 15b, 17t; **TopFoto.co. uk**: 23cr; **USGS**: 54, 55l; **Vireo**: 32fcla.

Map
FLPA: William S. Clark 2bl; **naturepl.com**: Richard Du Toit 2tl; **Photoshot/NHPA**: Andrea Bonetti 1crb; Robert Erwin 2tc; Mike Lane 1cla; MLA001909A 1clb; Roger Tidman 2tr; Alan Williams 1bl, 2br; **U.S.F.W.S**: 1cra, 1fbr, 1fcra.

Profiles
See Page 16 of *Bird Profiles*

Wall chart
See Page 72 of *Eyewitness Bird*

Clip-art CD
See the *Credits* file on the CD

All other images © Dorling Kindersley
For further information see:
www.dkimages.com

The publisher would also like to thank:
Ed Merritt for cartography on the Map; **Ben Hoare** and **Carey Scott** for additional writing; **Polly Boyd** for proofreading; **Hilary Bird** for the index; **Neil Lockley** and **Lisa Stock** for editorial assistance; and **Margaret Parrish** for Americanization.